MILITARY VEHICLES
ABRAMS TANKS

BY JOHN HAMILTON

VISIT US AT
WWW.ABDOPUBLISHING.COM

Published by ABDO Publishing Company, 8000 West 78th Street, Suite 310, Edina, MN 55439. Copyright ©2012 by Abdo Consulting Group, Inc. International copyrights reserved in all countries. No part of this book may be reproduced in any form without written permission from the publisher. A&D Xtreme™ is a trademark and logo of ABDO Publishing Company.

Printed in the United States of America, North Mankato, Minnesota.
042011
092011

Editor: Sue Hamilton
Graphic Design: Sue Hamilton
Cover Design: John Hamilton
Cover Photo: U.S. Army
Interior Photos: Department of Defense-pgs 2, 3, 6, 7, 9, 12, 13, 20, 24, 25, 26, 27, 30, 31 & 32; Getty Images-pgs 8, 18 & 19; United States Army-pgs 4, 5, 9 (inset), 10, 11, 13 (left & right inset), 14, 15, 16, 17 & 28; United States Marines-pgs 1, 17, 19 (inset), 21, 22, 23, & 29.

Library of Congress Cataloging-in-Publication Data

Hamilton, John, 1959-
  Abrams tanks / John Hamilton.
      p. cm. -- (Military vehicles)
  Includes index.
  ISBN 978-1-61783-073-0
  1. M1 (Tank)--Juvenile literature. I. Title.
  UG446.5.H28 2011
  623.7'4752--dc22
                    2011015971

TABLE OF CONTENTS

ABRAMS MAIN BATTLE TANK ★★★

The Abrams is the United States Army's main battle tank. It is highly mobile and heavily armored. It attacks enemy forces using powerful weapons. The Abrams tank is one of the Army's most fearsome tools on today's battlefield.

XTREME FACT

The Abrams tank has advanced armor. During the 1990-91 Persian Gulf War, not a single Abrams tank crewman was killed in the conflict.

ABRAMS TANK HISTORY

The Abrams tank was developed in the 1970s to replace the United States military's aging M60 battle tank. The Abrams is faster, has better armor, and superior firepower. The first M1 Abrams tank entered service in 1980.

An M1 Abrams main battle tank in 1983.

XTREME FACT

The Abrams tank is named after General Creighton Williams Abrams Jr., who commanded the U.S. Army in the Vietnam War from 1968 to 1972.

ABRAMS TANK VERSIONS

The M1 Abrams had a 105mm main gun. It was built from 1979 to 1985.

The M1A1 Abrams tank was built from 1985-1993. It was fitted with a more powerful 120mm smoothbore cannon, plus improved armor.

An M1 Abrams with a 105mm main gun.

The modern M1A2 Abrams includes hi-tech sensors, navigation systems, and fire-control computers.

An M1A1 Abrams main battle tank lays a smoke screen.

M1A2 with TUSK (Tank Urban Survival Kit) for urban battle

Remote Weapons Station

Loader's Armor Gun Shield

Loader's Thermal Sight

Tank/Infantry Telephone

Thermal Sight Goggles

Rear Protecting Unit Slat Armor

Thermal Sight Components

Abrams Reactive Armor Tiles

9

ABRAMS TANK
FAST FACTS

M1A2 Abrams Tank Specifications

Length:	32 feet (9.7 m)
Width:	12 feet (3.7 m)
Height:	8 feet (2.4 m)
Weight:	68 tons (61.7 metric tons)
Top Speed:	42 miles per hour (67.6 kph)
Cruising Range:	275 miles (443 km)
Crew:	4
Main Weapon:	120mm smoothbore cannon
Manufacturer:	General Dynamics
Replacement Cost:	$4.3 million

XTREME FACT

There are about 4,796 Abrams tanks in the United States arsenal (4,393 Army and 403 Marine Corps).

CREW

The M1A2 Abrams has a crew of four, including a tank commander, a driver, a gunner, and an ammunition loader.

Gunner

Tank Commander

Driver

Loader

GIT DRIVE ACTIVE   MASTER   PANEL DIM   RESET   MASTER
HATCH OPEN   CAUTION   WARNING

ARMOR

Abrams tanks are very hard to destroy. They are protected by layers of steel, ceramics, plus high-strength plastics and fibers, such as Kevlar. Explosive reactive armor detonates on contact, decreasing the effectiveness of enemy anti-tank weapons.

XTREME FACT

Modern tanks are more heavily armored toward the front of the vehicle.

CANNON

The main weapon of the M1A2 Abrams is a 120mm smoothbore cannon. It can fire high-velocity rounds that penetrate the armor of enemy tanks. The Abrams can also attack enemy troops, or even low-flying aircraft.

An Abrams main battle tank fires a 120mm round.

The view from behind the 120mm cannon on an Abrams tank.

FIRE CONTROL

Advanced fire-control systems allow the Abrams to hit targets even when dashing over rough ground. Thermal vision sights and laser rangefinders allow gunners to see targets at night, or in dusty, smoky battlefield conditions.

An Abrams hits targets in rough, dusty conditions.

An Abrams tank and crewman as seen through the thermal imaging sights of another tank.

OTHER WEAPONS

In addition to its main cannon, the Abrams is armed with a .50-caliber heavy machine gun and two 7.62mm machine guns. The tank is also equipped with smoke grenade launchers.

Soldiers man a M2 .50-caliber machine gun (left) and a M240 7.62mm machine gun (right).

A tank crewman braces himself after firing from the turret.

ENGINE

The Abrams M1A2 tank is powered by a 1,500-horsepower turbine engine. It can run on diesel, kerosene, or gasoline fuel. Even though the Abrams is a very heavy tank, it has a top speed of 42 miles per hour (67.6 kph).

Soldiers work on a 1,500-horsepower air-gas turbine engine from an M1A1 Abrams.

The Abrams tank is a gas guzzler. It travels about .6 miles (1 km) per gallon of fuel.

XTREME FACT

Repairs complete, the powerful engine is lowered back into an Abrams tank.

CONVENTIONAL WARFARE

On the battlefield, the Abrams tank is one of the most formidable weapons in the world. It uses superior firepower, maneuverability, and armored protection to defeat almost any enemy, in any weather, day or night.

Morning patrol in Fallujah, Iraq.

XTREME FACT

Advanced air filters protect the crew from most chemical or biological attacks.

URBAN WARFARE

Tanks are more vulnerable to attack when fighting in cities or other urban areas. The Abrams M1A2 can be outfitted with a Tank Urban Survival Kit (TUSK). It includes improved side and rear armor, plus shielding to protect turret gunners.

An Abrams tank fires against enemy forces in Fallujah, Iraq.

OTHER MISSIONS

The M104 Wolverine is a modified Abrams tank with a portable bridge instead of a turret. The bridge can be assembled in less than five minutes, and can support heavy armored vehicles.

XTREME
FACT

To detonate mines, an Assault Breacher Vehicle shoots out a rocket with a long string of C4 explosives.

The M1 Assault Breacher Vehicle clears paths for troops and other vehicles through enemy minefields. It uses a heavy plow or line explosives to detonate mines. It has been used by the U.S. Marine Corps in Afghanistan.

GLOSSARY

AMMUNITION

The bullets and shells used in weapons.

ARMOR

A strong, protective covering made to protect military vehicles.

ARSENAL

A collection of guns usually owned by a military group or country.

DIESEL FUEL

A thick petroleum product that is used in diesel engines, such as those found in heavy tanks or trucks.

GRENADE

A bomb with a delayed explosion thrown by hand or shot from a rifle or launcher.

KEROSENE

A fuel oil used in tanks and jet engines. It is also used for heat and light in some homes.

Kevlar

A light and very strong man-made fiber. It is used to make helmets, vests, and other protective gear for military and law enforcement personnel.

M60 Patton Tank

A steel-armored main battle tank first introduced in 1960.

Navigation System

A computer and satellite system that provides directions and locations.

Persian Gulf War

A war fought from 1990-1991 in Iraq and Kuwait between the forces of Iraq's President Saddam Hussein and a group of United Nations countries led by the United States.

Smoothbore Cannon

A cannon whose barrel has a smooth interior, instead of spiraled grooves.

Thermal Imaging

Equipment that uses an object's warmth to obtain an image.

Turret

The top part of a tank, which houses the main cannon and other weapons. The turret rotates, allowing a gunner to aim and fire in any direction.

Vietnam War

A conflict between the countries of North Vietnam and South Vietnam from 1955-1975. Communist North Vietnam was supported by China and the Soviet Union. The United States entered the war on the side of South Vietnam.

INDEX

RENEW ONLINE AT *WITHDRAWN*
www.glencoepubliclibrary.org
select "My Library Account"
OR CALL 847-835-5056

DATE DUE

MAY 1 1 2015	
JAN - 2 2016	
FEB - 4 2016	
JUL 1 1 2017	
JUL - 9 2018	
AUG - 8 2018	
SEP - 5 2018	
AUG 1 0 2021	
JUN 2 4 2023	
	PRINTED IN U.S.A.